Critical Acclaim

"Bernadette Dyer is a folk singer of the Caribbean and a weaver of fantastic, moral and spellbinding tales. Her words induct and seduce, instruct and soothe. Elementary in style, but philosophical in subject, she be Miss Lou at song and Aesop at the story telling. To open her books is to be enlightened, and one closes them knowing one has been refreshed and improved."

- George Elliott Clarke, internationally renowned poet, Parliamentary Poet Laureate of Canada

"...a wonderful collection of stories that have common universal themes in a multicultural context. The themes of love, identity, tradition versus modern beliefs are woven well in stories... with unpredictable endings."

- Karen Lemmons, Goodreads book reviewer

"...a beautiful piece of literary art. Richly written, Dyer takes the reader on an historical trip through World war I and the Holocaust. She eases the reader from one cultural experience to the next with ease and grace. With each page the reader is captivated ... If you are in to quality, no nonsense fiction...Bernadette Gabay Dyer is your writer."

- T. Rhythm Knight, Apoo Bookclub

" Bernadette Gabay Dyer ...brings a unique voice influenced by the Caribbean experience and sSto-

rytelling tradition to the Canadian Diaspora in ways that unite cultures and foster insight and understanding."

- Nicole Lyn, Actress & Celebrity

"The sometimes whimsical, sometimes mystical. sometimes nostalgic, always poignant collection of short stories is definitely more than "fair". Bernadette Dyer skillfully navigates the immigrant experience, which is the common thread that weaves its way through this great collection. Its colourful characters grab hold of your heart, and leave you wanting more. ...Ms. Dyer's voice is obviously steeped in memory, passion, and a rich and diverse family history. which act as jumping off points for her vivid imaginings, which shares with us in brilliant detail. A definitive MUST read for short story lovers."

- Cheryl Philips, author, book reviewer

"Bernadette Gabay Dyer has made her indelible mark on Canadian letters with her novels, stories and poems as well as a storyteller. ..Her literary work reveals her commitment to exposing world rooted in her unforgettable Caribbean heritage. She is truly a writer dedicated to continuous exploration of new narrative strategies and new themes that harness the power of seeing the world through different and caring eyes. Regardless of genre, she is, above all, a masterful storyteller."

Olive Senior, Award-Winning Author, of fiction, non-fiction, poetry, children's books.

Stone Woman

Stone Woman

Poems

Bernadette Gabay Dyer

Library and Archives Canada Cataloguing in Publication

Title: Stone woman / Bernadette Gabay Dyer.

Names: Dyer, Bernadette, author.

Description: Poems.

Identifiers: Canadiana (print) 20210383305 |
Canadiana (ebook) 20210383313 |

9781771616164 (softcover) | ISBN 9781771616171 (PDF) |
ISBN 9781771616188 (EPUB) | ISBN 9781771616195 (Kindle)

Classification: LCC PS8557.Y47 S76 2021 | DDC C811/.54—dc23

Published by Mosaic Press, Oakville, Ontario, Canada, 2022.

MOSAIC PRESS, Publishers
www.Mosaic-Press.com

Copyright © Bernadette Gabay Dyer 2022

Printed and bound in Canada

MOSAIC PRESS
1252 Speers Road, Units 1 & 2, Oakville, Ontario, L6L 5N9
(905) 825-2130 • info@mosaic-press.com • www.mosaic-press.com

Dedications for Stone Woman

These poems are dedicated to three poets who
encouraged my creativity
James Deahl, George Elliott Clarke & Al Moritz
Diana Fitzgerald Bryden and Carol Barbour

Acknowledgements

Thanks to Composer David Jaeger who set my, poem Dancing in the Sand, to music

Thanks to my friend Karen Usha, an accomplished soprano, who sang Dancing in the Sand

Thanks to my long time multi talented friend, and fellow creative, Carol Barbour, who always encouraged me.

Thanks to Rochelle Pangilinan for her patience in typing my manuscript

Thanks to Honey Novick, Poet

Thanks to Karen Gray, Vocalist

Table of Contents

POEMS

Love Spell

Fearing the sound of your
Retreating footsteps,
I have tied your secret name
Into seventeen knots in string,
Each to bind your heart
With a blessing,
So that goodbyes will not
Trigger sorrowful echoes in the hall,
Echoes to outrun dreams
Like wild birds in flight
Awakening swarms of moths
That swoop from under night's hill,
To thrill against the needle
I placed through the red candlewick
That now glows in agonizing flames
To pierce
Your heart.

Kitchen Solitaire

I will not find you
In that house on Delaware
For its doors are barred and windows bolstered
Against intruders and the cold,
It is a lonely place now,
Drafts seep and sigh along the hardwood floors
And the kitchen where I once marveled at your practiced
    hands
Creating cuisines savory and spicy
Has become a place of solitude.
Tiles are curled and paint blistered,
Herbs abandoned hang from rafters on the ceiling,
Only silence lives there.
Blackened kettles and crusted pots
Wait in dank humidity
In corners where once I observed
Hot steam coiling from your soups and stews
While oil spluttered and sizzled in a frenzied dance
In the iron Dutch pot you so lovingly brought
Across the Nicaraguan border,
I will not forget how you lingered over the stove
Inhaling and savouring all those international flavours,
And even if I close my eyes against the memory,
I still will not find you there
Or hear your voice echoing in the empty halls
Of the kitchen solitaire
And I know, I will not find you,
Not even in the drizzled flakes
Of thyme, mint, and marjoram.

While Her Hours Wound Down

Her tasting tart apple spray
Awoke memories
Hidden deep inside her soul
Like the bitter tang of her existence
And how it hurt at the core
Where her belief that one a day
Would keep him away
Still lived,
And her resolve that in the end
She could wrestle death to its grave.
She the enigma, the conundrum, the mystic mystery
Defied solutions, freely mingled
Amongst the defiled, the abused, and the blameless,
And in her last hour, must have felt
The apple's red flames upon her cheek of unrequited love,
In the arms of a stranger, the construction worker
Who miraculously reminded her of a magician
Of her own creation, who held life and death in sway.
His heavy boots crudely laced, his rough hands
Smeared in Mother Earth
Brought a lump to her throat,
And his brown rounded biceps sun exposed
Startled her with their beauty,
When devilry in his eye
Caused her to reflect instead
On the exact azure blue shade of her bicycle
That with its borrowed wings
Flew her to where the wind floated
Like swarms of feathers
Through her unruly blue black hair

While she concentrated on the romance
Of trimming the vines and undergrowth
Of her secluded city garden,
That paradise where life like dying soldiers
Saluted with a pride gone yellow, gone slack.
Privy to cultivation growing wild
And drunk from bird's song.
She revelled in the sweet nectar
And braced herself against the pink door
The magical gateway
Through which flowed
Artists, poets, and musicians
Of her acquaintance
Who passionately drank
The debris of past celebrations
To once again regale her writing
While her hours wound down
Around her
And her pale creative hand
Obscured the rich dark midnight tones
That lingered in her hair
And careered across her reflective eyes
Eyes like those of her legions of cats.
She the psychic who knew dreams
Even before they came,
Never told him who she was
When together they trembled
At the potency of her poetry
While the apple's red
Reflected up into her snowy white face
To colour her phantom cheeks.

For The One I Love

I have fallen into the sun,
How I sizzle,
You, who are almost
Half my years
Know exactly how
To break me into loving bits
And stop my heart beating,
As I, in shivers
Drown again and again
In liquid ice,
As I fall
Into your flames.

An Apology

If I don't look,
I won't see you
Stumble,
And if I'm not there
To witness it,
You'll not
Grow old.

Calvary Coming?

No cavalry came
While stranded I tottered at the edge
Of security and sanctity
Lost on dreams,
The world shatters on my sleeve.
Nothing remains
But an old black cloud
Of residue
Damp dark and haunting
With the scream of silence
Echoing in all the quiet places
Where raised fists
Curse at the wind
For the cavalry has not come.

Morning Fire

Threatening Victoria
And Vancouver mornings,
You turn in your sleep
While your eyelids flutter
Against cheeks
That loved me,
Slate-coloured eyes
Set deep
Invite fearful kisses of reassurance
While my fingertips
Trace all your lines
Curves, nooks, and crannies
During your Okanagan sleep.

My Black Mother

Mother has seen
Two World Wars
Seen the world grow old,
Seen us grow from childhood
To adult, and us become parents ourselves,
Yet like a rock she clings
Watching us all through the marriages
That causes the family to become Japanese,
Italian, Chinese, Black, and Irish.
Death has eluded us all,
Mother's prayers keeps it at bay,
Keeps aeroplanes in the air when we fly,
Keeps the highway safe for us
Although her sure steps have become slow
Dragging painful ones,
And she cocks her head to one side in the manner of
    those
Devoid of perfect hearing and vision
And her back has begun to curve towards the self
She steadies with a shaky hand.

The Face On Mars

Hush,
Or she will not
Speak of her aloneness,
Or how her eyes
For all eternity
Must scan distances
Unfathomable,
And she will not let you
Hear the wailing
Of frigid razor-sharp
Winds
That lash her
Incessantly,
She will not speak
Of her dreams,
Lost for all millennia,
She will not reveal
Secrets hidden
In the massive
Granite slabs
Of the mountain range
That surrounds her.
Hush,
Or she will become
Unvoiced,
Silent and secretive,
She will not speak of
Being abandoned
Beneath the swirling stars,
Where like a goddess

With an Aegean face
She remains still,
So still,
Frozen for all time
In a dark red sea
Of loneliness.

Far Far From Home

Don't listen to my heart
It drums disconsolately
And like the wind
Chases dreams.
It cannot find rest,
Not even when streets magically merge at Huron,
Where the eagle's son
Arms held wide, soars unflinchingly
Directly into the sun,
To embrace unsurpassed brilliance
He the obliterator of my wanting
Can still tears sharp as thorns,
Stay loneliness, despair, and elusive dreaming
Far far from home.
Would that angels with dust upon their feet
Could confine all broken promises, to lost dreams.
And sweeten tongues
Darkened in fallacy,
And would that they be then enticed
To dwell in this abode of sorcery
This common ground, dug deep in reverence
Where a woman with spirals in her ears
Claimed once to have loved,
Far far from home.

Distancing

Mathias, have you thought of me this night
While alone in your room you meditate
On the resonance of one note, and how profoundly it can
reverberate
And raise your consciousness
Above the reality of the seeping cold invading your win-
dow panes,
Tormenting with icy chills, and bitter loneliness.
I wonder if you ever clutch at memories we collected like
jars of coins
Throughout all these years,
Or if when you glance over at that corner
Where we often left our clothes,
Do you see me standing there, statue-still, awaiting and
wanting you,
And wonder if I still care
Even after your insistence on distancing yourself
For a chance to breathe and be confined from the city's
confusion.
And now that you are free, with a thousand chances at
departing
Do you still feel obliged to start afresh
And forget that I too lost out at elusive games.
And there are times when forgetting the rules you imposed
I still feel the sensation of your chest heaving
And listen to the hollow sound of your breathing,
And your inner voice speaking.
Be not fearful, it will say, you can always find someone else
to love.
And Mathias, I shudder against myself in a profusion of
tears,

And when you are solitary, indulging in self-examination
    and recrimination
Beside your green bowl of perfectly formed pears
Placed exactly where the last rays of evening sun
Will find them drape din your damp handkerchief,
Kissed up against the neck of your bass guitar,
Do life's bell-curves of memories
Forever lead you back to me, or are you still wanting
Always to concentrate only on yoga postures
And the voice of our Lord speaking,
And Mathias, does he tell you, of my desires too.

Lonely Room

Went into your room
Knowing you wouldn't be there
Saw where you left your boots, shoes
And clothes crumpled under the window
Where light filtering in silently picked out
Dust particles, and the rich burgundy tones
Of your Persian rug.
How often have I seen you standing there
Feet bare,
Playing wondrous tunes
For no one to hear.
Your music stand and rolled futon
Seem strangely lonely now
In a room so bare
Where only muted light
From behind bamboo shades
Peeps in,
Wanting to play
While you are away.

Needing Air

Have you seen the crone who sits in the shadows,
That old sage wrinkled and wise
Who cringes at the red candles' burning,
Her hidden name must be patience,
She will not be appeased,
I have seen her through smiles, and through tears,
She has waited for as long as memory
And lovingly carries a silken shroud
Her gift from the dark side,
Woven from a bouquet of sad black roses;
I am needing air,
Can you hear her bones,
They creak and cry out
As ominously as an icy wind along an icy shore,
She creeps inside my skin,
The years let her in,
And leaves me shivering
I need air for breathing,
Though the flickering red candle's flame
Burns low, burns tears that rage against the warm breath
That wrestles death
In its embers.

After We Were Gone

The house stands lonely
At the kilter in the avenue,
Its large wooden door of solitude
Beckons welcome half-heartedly,
Painted with tarnished memories.
By the lush bay windows
Laced in ivy
Your face, pale even in the half light
Watches our car disappear
Into pinpoint,
Twirling our victories and defeats,
Trembling your knitting needle-like fingers,
Against your jutting chin,
And tracing lines
Etched there by
Your ninety years.

The Domino Players

I cannot forget Horace's house
Sitting lonely on a hill,
Where shades of magenta and cadmium wink
From lush pepper fields that sweep
Down towards a large rocky walled-in garden
That hosts shy roses of white and pink
And a stark surprise of belled alamanders
The colour of marigolds
All aflutter atop a crest that dips
Down to green-brown furrowed fields
That seem seductively to peep from that lofty elevation
At the distant sea.
And it is a place where horses are tethered
In faery wooded compounds
Not far from the concrete parapets
That stand as solid as granite stone,
In a blaze of white sunlight
That cannot reach the cool secluded shades
Beneath the lignum vitae trees,
Which stand guard by the meshed in patios,
The rambling verandahs,
Surrounding that wayfaring home
That creaks and leans into the wind
With an air of welcoming,
And a grace dwarfed only by
The hardy hibiscus flowers that cluster round
And flaunt their scarlet beauty like whores,
All rivalling to compete
With the cries, the slaps, the whipping down
Of "hard cards," the dominoes,

Whose terrible smacks and powerful whacks go
Against the heart, the breast of my memories,
And the players whose raucous shouts obliterate
The surrounding wonder.

The Tenant Below

From the floor below
I can almost hear you squirming in your clothes
And know how deliciously you long
To explode the venom
Of your complaints
As you pace the floor
And cross and criss-cross the ceiling
Where your thoughts bore through
The peeling paint
And circle the tensioned air
Which pounds upon my waiting and wanting
To protect myself from your silver, vicious, velvet tongue
And I will not be absorbed by the weight
The silences or the screaming.
Shut off in my world, I'll breathe
And cut the umbilical slowly.

Masks

It is not exile that holds me here,
Not a dance of the divined,
The pain that injects my soul is impatient
And wordless as indecision,
It is the dreaming in this alien existence
Inside days of bitter cold,
That seeps like icy breath
Beneath windowsills
Billowing the winding sheets
Of tormented hostility.
It is a slow death, slow derision
That glints from your eyes
Where masks alone hides and disguises the outward anxiety
Which temporarily shields the self
That bleeds.

Primordial Morning

We are fragile,
No further ahead
Than the ferns that rustled
On the dawning of a
Primordial morning.
Eggshell thin, we breathe in air
Which scorches our existence.
How brittle we still are,
After years of shattering our pasty bones
On harsh words and innuendo,
Like withered vines, creeping
And brown
Choking forests from the light
We straddle the tiny crawling things,
Who like us must still
Gasp for air
Amidst struggling ferns.

Reflections

Lazarus rises swiftly
Leaving us behind frozen wheels of forgiveness,
His snowy hands chases us through streets of horror
Then abandons us as we grieve
At the helm of disasters not yet come,
He binds us under the weight of forgotten remembrances
Of times when he once stood at Bathurst and Bloor
Laconic and nomadic,
Hair washing over the eyes
That reflect my private pain.
Lazarus' outstretched hand
Dances in the limpid air
Awaking mirrors in his mind
To reflect my shame, my silence, my menacing.
Faceless he stands against city crowds
Hair fluttering against eyes impossibly brilliant
Mumbling blind apologies.

On College Street

I, a dying lily
Am limp
Unable to tread
The shallow waters
That surround you
Or surmount verbal barriers
Razor sharp
That dance in your air.
How dangerously close
I waltz with death,
Its sweet perfume engulfs me
And dissolves and intoxicates,
As I in alpha state refuse
To acknowledge
Even the busty women in black stockings
Who pine for you
While they hide behind the blazing lights of Café
    Diplomatico,
As I reverse on the speeding wheels
Of my determination
To die in your company,
Enthralled by markings on your palms
That will show signs that you are claimed
Even the fountain of prune-coloured hair
That cascades upon your evening face,
Where shards of dim light shield
Pearl like tears that streak
In the sooty fall hours on College Street.

You And I

Do you not remember
The passion now spent
Which lashed across lakes
Blinding us in the face of misty noon-day splendour
Causing our fingers to grasp
One another as though
For the last time, for the first time
While forgetting the dreams
We carved in the buckling confines
Of rooming house walls
Impervious to the ravishing kisses
We set adrift on a whistling wind
Which caressed all the flagging leaves of summer
And plumped up every blade of downy grass,
There, for our sake
Atop the Shakespearian hills of High Park
No, only in jest, you forget
Our double images
Repeated in the silent waters
Inspiring our sneak peeks at selves
Reflected in windows flashing by.

Mysterious One

You, like the last of the tigers
Peer through stripes
That straddle the borders of dreams
Into wizened smile,
And ancient eyes that blaze
As they watch for death
Flaunting false security in your presence,
Stripe atop stripe
Darting against light
Opening abysses as black as your eyes
Where fate snatches us from behind
Keeping us safe as it were in its cutglass edge
Which stifles passion when
White hot lips brush
Against fangs.

Looking Back

In times past, I followed
Your sure-footed lead
Through dust and undergrowth,
Slipped amongst ferns,
Grazed my heels atop high places,
Blistered my fingers
One after another,
Until like a slow erosion of soil
My faith wore thin
Leaving my eyes unfocused
In strange dimness.
Now at long last
With spirit broken,
I lay prostrate
In a bluey haze
Unable to breathe
Your remembrance.

Before English Come

God does not hear our prayers,
Concrete and steel prevent his listening,
Even when with lost dignity
We beg twenty cents
On subway platforms and moving trains
Where suspicious passengers
Asian, African, Indian, and Middle Easterners eye us
And look past us as though
We are not really there.
Smiling inside themselves,
European imagine us only as children
In need of harsh discipline.
God does not hear our words,
For how else could he forget
Our brave ancestors
Who stood on this very soil
Before English come
To this land, our country
Where our gods once could be heard
In the north wind's harsh whistle
Blowing through the drifting snow
And in the roar of summer thunder,
Our gods no longer answer our prayers,
We are outcasts
Unable to hear their voices
As we hustle the twenty cents from strangers
Who cannot hear the pain in our throats,
Or understand our territorial recognition
Of this our beloved Kanata,
Where the steel train's roar
Fills us with a violent thunder

That echoes our ancestral names
Through the long dark tunnels between stations
Where no one seems to remember
That so few of us are left
So few,
For there were more than fifty tribes of us
And more than fifty native tongues
Before English come.

Black Woman Talk To Me

Who is that ugly black woman
That stares out at me
With skin loose and wrinkled
Exposing eyes that once shone bright,
And a mouth once curiously soft and light with kisses,
Who is she with the straggly hair,
Hair that used to be so daringly dark and lush,
Had she ever been pretty I wonder,
Who is she,
She who is so silent
Eyes bright with harsh stares
And lips that only move
When I move mine.

The Abductors

From a door in the air, they silently come
Like angels on gossamer feet
A band of silver entities,
Those abductors, those alien beings
With humming and buzzing sounds
Soft as silence,
Potent as stings,
In full disguise, frail, and spindly
On light feet they'll march
To reach us in our beds.
Their large eyes will mesmerize,
Do not be deceived, be warned!
For when they frequent dwelling places
In that nocturnal time of perfect harmony
Between sleep and wakefulness,
Darkness and the dawning,
When we are most vulnerable
When we are alone,
They'll come ...
Those terrorists, those renegades
Their true strength revealed,
And there is no escaping them
No matter how hard you plead!
They are small,
Barely four feet tall,
Moving as one body, one mind,
Ignoring your screaming,
And no one will hear

When they take you to where
There is a door in the air
Where angels appear
To watch over you.

Stone Woman

She will not show her face
It is a solemn one
That hides behind a waterfall
Of tears.
Her trampled heart
Falls out windows,
Dying repeatedly from dawn until dusk,
And in the rare moments
Of your presence
Is reduced to rubble
For her granite stoic concerns dissolve
Into infinite excuses
For your absences,
The holes you leave in the air
Your dizzying minefield of obligations
As you work late in restaurants
Preparing lunches for Ottawa girls
Who thrive on cubed melon slices,
A Mayan vision, and meetings
That aid in editing outtakes from food bank rushes,
Films that freeze time against frames, against tears
As you analyze Macbeth, an intrigue of language
And Henry V, a seduction of your senses
Before relations form Banff
Arrive in Richmond Hill
To demand undivided attention,
While she, a statue waxen
Bleeds alone, with candle incantations,
Smudge sticks, herbs,
And tumbled stones.

Slowly

Slowly, slowly,
Breathing in slowly
While the patterns of my life spin by,
Going slowly,
Taking my own time
Getting stuck in your mind,
Staying there,
Remembering our tears
Can almost taste them in the air
Drifting weightless like feathers
Falling slowly.
Slowly, slowly,
Exchanging a smile,
Experiencing a shiver,
A slow one,
From here on in
Facing the world with a grin,
But going slowly.

Freedom Tears

Africa laughs from my eyes
Tinges my blood purple,
Curls my hair at the roots,
Denies me a future solitude
By chaining me darkly to the past,
She cries out to me of hope
Oh Africa,
You relish my salty
Freedom tears,
And coil like a serpent
Forever waiting
For the child who still
Has not come home.

The Idol With The Gabriel Face

You are out of the country,
Yet I feel unspeakably close
I look at photographs, and wonder,
Do birds chirping at windows not know
That you are not here,
Or are they like me
At a loss for words to express
Emptiness.
I had almost lost hope,
Even as I waited for the ink to dry
On the many unopened letters
I sent to you,
But my spirit is not broken,
Though I once searched for you
In the quick glint of cigarette light,
And touched my hands
In imagination
Against your angelic Gabriel face,
And knew even then
That in dim cafes and bars
Everyone else owns you,
Even the flickering darkness
Imprisons you in brilliance
Despite the glistening in the light that lives
In the long lines of your stage clothes.
Incandesce serves only to hide your face in pallor
Pales as impending death
Where no votive with its veil
Obscures those of us too shy
To shine in liquid chains of desire,

As I, mesmerized by you,
Strive to render impotent
Stares and tears of all those others
Who would dare adore you,
As I, unrivalled stand
Amidst your flames.

Your Mother And The River

Your mother's potent prayers could have
Harnessed the meandering river where we waded last sum-
    mer,
Could have silenced that babbling waterway
That now hurries headlong
Amongst weeds and giant rocks charging into the wild
    country
That you have grown accustomed to.
It must have been her calloused hands, her bruised palms
That afforded a path for us
As her impassioned tears washed away
The undertow, the mud, the silt.
And she must have caused the skies to be painted
In colours we barely understood
Colours that intruded even into our hiding places
Revealing hasty greens, indomitable blues and shy purples
Where jagged stones glistened
Like strands of scattered pearls in the palm of the sun,
And we are eagerly draw to such places
Sensing her elusive presence
Even in the secret caves and the tiny flowers that grown
Profusely along the shores
Of the mighty Rio Cobra.

Let Him Sleep

He comes,
A child
Call him Jorge
A dream name,
A naked one
With scents of papaya, avocado, and cocoa
To colour him.

He thrives,
Thrives on milk drawn
From the udders of a she-goat,
His history carved
On the belly of the impatient wind,
For only the wind knows
The wild uncultivated land that stretches
Far outside of Lima,
And knows the taste of salty tears
Tears that jewel
The rushing waters of the Amazon.

And it knew Juanita Gomez
Her screams,
Her open mouth of pain,
That let the night in,
It knew her thighs that raged
Form his birthing,
And the terror that bit and bit again
As she writhed
When the unforgiving night told her of him,
Before she slept forever,

Leaving him beside her
Where he lay iridescent and glistening
In rude sheets that could not hide the beauty
Exposed in the curve of his heel, his cheek
Inviting unsuspecting adoration,
As he breathe in the arms of moonlight,
Innocent, cold, and playful.

How easy to have snuffed him out,
With no whisper of his existence
But no ...

Set the candle of the world
Once more to blazing
On the windowsill of time.
It is a sign, send word,
The baby lives!
Perfect fingers, toes, a warm haunting beauty.
Call him Jorge, it is a name for the fullness of life.

Bring a soft basket to cradle him,
A basket woven by the hands of a virgin at midnight,
Set a straw stuffed pillow at his head,
Put the umbilical in a muslin bag near him,
Place a veil of fresh chicken skin over his tender lips,
So that nothing impure will pass over to him.
Then catch his dreams in the cage of woven reeds
At his resting head.

Let him sleep.
Gather all his dreams,
He is a sweet nectar in the bitter night,
Try not to be entranced by him,
For the red that rushes in his veins

Is like addictive wine,
It binds the vines, the trees, and the scarlet trumpet lilies
That foreshadow gloom, sorrow, and impending death.
The blue feathered veins at his neck
Speak of tenderness.
Be wary,
For if by chance he opens his eyes
The darkness will escape
Out into the blackness, the exact shade
Of the underside of a bat's wing.

Hush! His lips flutter like butterflies
Even in sleep,
His nostrils quiver
Like gentle jungle flowers
His small hands brush against the air like leaves
His heart beats a tattoo as black as night's drummer.

O, such sweetness is surely a curse
For all womankind.
His legs are as strong
As a mountain goat's
His hair blue-black and furious.

Already his belly is sensuously flat,
He walks upright!
Straining always for the unreachable
While hating Juanita for abandoning him.
Look, the quicksilver of his lips
Curves in and out of smiles,
And he grows,
Watch him!
Pray he never crosses oceans,
For his swollen malevolent dreams

Explode like shooting stars.
No reed basket, cassava leaf bed, or palm-lined huts,
Or village can contain him.

His woman love, and his rage
Disguised as well-learned manners
Walk with him into the future
Unconstrained,
He comes ...

Old Woman Things

You must not have heard me
On the stairs
For all its creaking and sighs, so like yours
Expressed through the years.
It must have been my stocking feet
Soft against your listening
In these winter years,
For you were not aware of me
Fighting against welling tears
That threatened to dissolve my resolve
To be strong there on the landing
Where your room in full view
Afforded a glimpse of pale sunlight
That played upon your hair and face
Painting you angelic, childlike, and translucent
In a silver haze,
As hunched over in your soft chair,
Lost in concentration
You sat there and attended
To old woman things.

The Sieve

Mama's eyes are distant now,
Pale, lost with flecks of brown.
Deep inside herself she goes
Where her fingers
In their fumblings
Are finding remembering,
Drumming out yesterdays
Elusive, unattainable
And flowing into the meagre
Suppers split five ways.
Riveted she sits in her corner
Unmindful
Of the uproarious laughter
She used to use
To fill each crack
And gaping hole in
Our crumbling walls.
No light guides her
Stooping shoulders,
No healing hidden in the kisses
She scatters
Into our parched existence.
She cries stains
Into an old grey jacket
Hanging at the door.

Weak Links

You left on a Thursday afternoon in February,
A long black limousine pulled out
As sunlight crept in
Through the window
Where you used to hide behind blinds,
And now we are afraid
That we will be expected to be strong
Though we are the weakest links
With ready tears to spill,
Tears that blinds us to malevolence
As we at your feet
Had admired your kindness,
And in our shame, called to mind
People that you did not forget,
People whose hopes you carried
Like pebbles in a handkerchief,
Though your listening ear
Had been dry from straining
Against their pleadings,
And you would not let us bear the pain,
Even as together we watched
For the horseman's coming.

Lynn: The Voice Inside

Don't wound me,
My heart is vulnerable
Although I carry stones inside my jaws,
And my teeth gnash against bullets
From the stares that will not rest easy inside my soul.
Keep your distance, your communions, for if you come
    closer
You will know who I really am.
Respect this privacy, these wounded pieces, these scars that
    bleed into scabs
And cover thin ankles, throat, and wrists with wanting
A fighting chance for survival.
Once, I was witness to a slow dying,
A death that inflamed me, then made me strong, and I
    raged for life
Until now, my defenceless eyes betray the compassionate
    side
That I keep confidential
Even from the red flames, the purple cadmium stains
That leap form my hair
With its warnings, its signals of danger
And these daggers I taught my eyes to shoot
Hunt me down and haunt me yet,
My pliant frame, pencil thin
Must bear the pain, the turning round
Of my upside down moods that swing
Holding me up for scrutiny against
Your grasping and your wanting
To discover that I was that girl by the fence
Hiding behind eyes that never smiled, in a place
Where dreams get splattered,

And I am the one whose heels raced headlong
Down the hills of abandonment,
Then had to play-act at being strong and resilient, for the
    others
Who still don't know, that my sweaty palms, long gone
    cold
Betray my plight, my very fight, to belong.

Where Sunlight Dare Not Follow

The tattoo artist's children
Ungainly tattered
Shiver in coats and ragged boots
As they roam the streets by dark,
Eyes heavy with fire
Rib cages smouldering,
And in the beat of a heart
They are set to running
On their bare feet
That race the wind, regardless of weather,
Their hats pulled down
To shade eyes against sleep,
Against the dark needle's thrill
As joyously they chase dogs' tails
Through alleys and lanes
Where sunlight dare not follow,
The melancholy artist's daughters and wayward sons
Flash bright smiles that crack gaping holes in their jaws
To mark them indelible
Like their blue veined rememberings
Of indigo ink
That still lives
In the silky white of their skin.

In The Aftermath

Our names are secret,
Even from the man from Zaire
Who stealthily watches our gestures,
Our moving lips,
And hears our words tangled with sounds
That barricade and isolate, rich with a familiar
Unfamiliar,
And we will not let him in
Until we hear him, and no longer fear him,
His presence brings news form our ancestral home.
· His voice is soft,
It cascades as gently as petals,
Then meets with silences
As haunting as the dark stretches of water
Which separate our continental births,
Waters that divide us from her, our mother Africa,
Who is ripe, maternal, and calling,
Weary from waiting and wanting
To suckle and nurture us, "her outside children"
Who reciprocate her longings
To fill emptiness in our hearts, our souls,
And she is unmindful of the Jewish, East Indian,
Chinese, and European blood
Which over the passage of years
Jostles for attention
In our dark blue veins
Like interconnecting rivers
Where latent memories once shared
Lie buried in a cup of tears.

The Colours Of My Adopted Country

A view of scruffy backyards
Is all that's left
For these eyes that have seen
Mountains rise majestic
Beyond Montego bay
And glanced across green glades
Of a forgotten parish called
St. Thomas where the Johnson River flows
Slippery and silent
Into Serge Island which even now
Looms lonely in this intrusion
Seemingly caught in the cool embrace
And meanderings of ferngullys
And I am tortured by rememberings
Of the haggard palm strewn beaches
Of Roselle
Where legend is even now
Turned aside in my mind
By the blinding snows
Of this my adopted country.

The Actor

Battle scarred and affection starved
I thoughtlessly intruded into your walled-in world
Selfishly insensitive to your dreaming
I am a stranger here, I heard myself say
Standing amidst the disjointed day
That flows from your heart
Entrapping others like myself
Who flounder by.
It is astute, alien, and psychic
This silence that exudes so menacingly,
I should have respected the cage you so carefully constructed
To contain your heart.
Alone I stand in your empty garden
Eyes downcast and shuddering
Because I never really knew you
Not even after we pondered over Martin Amis
Then traded stories,
Mine you have forgotten, I suppose,
But yours I remember:
Your teenage niece's New Year's Party
And how she acted more responsible and mature than
    expected.
Was it because of my impulsive laughter
That you thought I danced on the eggshells of your soul?
You couldn't have known that in reality
I fell apart at the heel and shank
Like a dying thoroughbred
Twirling my "might have beens"
Haunted by stories you told of a disturbed young man
Who hearing of your sister's pregnancy
Committed suicide!

It was his child wasn't it, and she his psychotherapist?
Is that why you could only hold me momentarily
As though refusing small comfort
Saying you were busy, had things to do,
A place to tidy, lines to learn
No more waiting in the wings
For you are an actor ... And your lonely garden beckons.

Night Journey

Daddy, I remember the white pools of light
Your car made against the blanket of night,
Lights that were all at once intrusive and protective
Veering along the unbearable lonely country roads
Leading to St. Thomas,
Roads that seemed strangely alive
Like serpents
Carved in strangle hold
Along treacherous mountain passes,
Holding us in a grip of memories.
I hide myself in the concealing spray of rocks and gravel
Whose living voices ping and zing against the rough metal
    of our car.
Coercing us to forget to remember
These landmarks, these dangerous curves
That lead us back home
With only the passage of years
To guide us where your footfalls even now falter against
Floor boards, echoing again and again your loneliness
Since we left you behind.
And Daddy, this night will not end
This isolation so grey, so desolate
Held up for scrutiny in your headlights
Attracting flying insects to freeze against the beams
And drowning the baying tongue of the night
Where thorny bushes sway
Under pinpointed sky
Denying the authority given by our lost civilization,
Daddy you must have seen it too
Seen the sad eyes, the haunted faces of the night children

Who fearlessly brush up against our moving vehicle,
Tempting fate, naming us moving targets
Beneath the sliver of moon
That moves mysteriously against the forested night.
It is a homecoming, Daddy,
The greening I have seen in your eyes.

The Unknown Field-Hand

He is there
In the recesses of my memory,
In half-forgotten landscapes
Craggy, ancient, and weather-beaten,
And he is there,
There with the sugarcane,
Dark as an ackee seed,
His lips purple as evening hibiscus
In the dying sun.
He stands against the gnarled yam hills
Etched in sunset hues
That spill over woody tamarind trees
Painted fiery orange and gold
He stands beside blackened palms
And green banana plantations,
Sinewy feet stoically planted
In dusty soil that whispers only to him
Words that catch in his parched throat,
Of ancestral retrospection, more ancient than these fields,
The craggy rocks, and even the thorny shame old lady
    weeds
That await rain.

Library Corners

It is a day of hooligans
Drunks, pushers, and pimps,
It is a day for bleeding.
The grey carpet seeps dark stains
That spreads under doors,
Advances up walls
To shrug at our cautions,
Questions fill emergent air,
Innocent and intriguing
As the long-awaited call
From the threads of instrumentation
Criss-cross the air, against our breathing,
Misunderstandings makes fools of us all,
For mother tongues no longer prove reliable
In listening to humanities secret wisdom
Of rich solutions,
Piety is imperative in these walls
Where poised in self-imposed isolation
A black boy is reading.

Egg Shells On Her Face

Hers is a dark ancient beauty,
A coveted jewel
To rival the white northern sky
She walks the downtown Kenora streets
With hair long and dusky
Singing on the wind,
Her lips heavy and sensual
Curved in half smile
Seem to know
That the slightly eastward tilt of her chin
Reflects the rich black gold of her eyes,
Crimson is the colour she wears with pride
Like a badge of defiance
Against all the stares
Which trace her steps,
And wonder at the egg shells on her face,
While years of tribal heritage
Thunders in her strides.

Blithe Spirits

It is the year
That I turn seven,
The sky is raw with memory.
Fields beckon
But I cannot reach their bright ribbons,
Birds call from the slanting sky,
As the river jangles by.
My heart is heavy
In the solid presence
Of the banyan tree
Whose arial roots like a veil
Will hide all my tears,
For I will not let this be farewell
To Serge Island my home,
This abode of myth and memories
Has nurtured me,
Filled my thoughts with magical beings,
Brought quicksilver dreams
While I slept under its blazing stars
That trembled above nights' dark shelves,
And I, witness to blithe spirits
Barely concealed
In the palm of the East Wind's hand,
And one of those rare companions
Will guide my right hands' destiny,
Two will guide my left,
So that my heart will not forget this place,
Not even the taciturn motion
Of the mighty wheels of the estate factory
As eternally it pressed sugar from the cane,
For each rotation burned with remembrance

When I in a cradle of dark mahogany wooden slats
Listened out for the resonance, the riot of nights sounds
Made by insects up against the window's mesh
That looked out into the bowels of darkness

Stella In Nursing Home

She slips away from me
Even as I hold her in my gaze,
And hides her eyes behind a veil
Of unshed tears.
She twists her frail frame
Into fetal positions
Allows herself to cry out
In silent screams
The self same questions
We mouth on damp lips.

What is this thing called life
Which in the end holds nothing
But a hollow cup?

Her knees and forehead meet
Between sheets
Which protect her from the hurts
We have tried to shield her from
With our velvet hands.

For Gwendolyn Macewen

If you can hear me
Take my hands
Speak through my pen
Mesmerize,
Take fabulous journeys
With Noman, Everyman
Make our lives a rich incantation
With illusions created under
Julian's magical hands.
Show us the reeling light through the dark dark eyes
Of the Night Child,
And teach us how to sadly laugh like Kali,
And weep Jubelas' lost tears.
Where are you precious one,
The one who haunts our remembering, our dreams
My pen ...
Are you on some forgotten ferris wheel dancing
A mad swirling dance.
Teach our hesitant feet
To follow yours as though
Caught between two worlds
Kingsmere and there,
Fill our mouths with stars,
Our ears with fire.

The Spectre

The streetcar is moving
It is as if I am dreaming,
My head rests on your shoulders Mama,
Is it too heavy, or am I light as air?
I see,
O Mama, I see through your eyes
The flashing by, the pulsing, the electric standards,
Plumbing shops, cafes, and variety stores.
I am almost ten
Yet I see your pain
Laid bare from remembrance of what we left behind
In El Salvador the land of our birth,
And it rises up at each curve like a spectre,
Calling and calling
Do not forget me, do not forget me.
And I in the secret splendour of your warm throat
And the softness of your Latin cheek
I am no longer just a boy
For I am magnificent in the unexplained joy of our close-
      ness
In this borrowed land.
O Mama, my eyes race along with yours
Like jaguars through these strange Toronto streets,
Streets cluttered with impenetrable concrete pointing at
      the sky.
And Mama, I hear the cries of the Condor, the Macaw,
And the wild Toucan.
My eyes swim with tears from our collective recollections

As we move along these streetcar lines,
These tracks that stretch like silver rail markings
Pointing our way
To unexplored places.

The Lake Remembers

The forest is silent
He is not there,
The Mestizo man
Who came from the mountains
And walked in the dark tangled foliage
Where birds now refuse to sing.
The forest is silent
It watches for him
Even in stagnant pools
Of Quechua and Aymara tears,
And it awaits him
In the green leafy valleys
That follow the passage of the sun
Out into the regions
Where the ink-dark lake
Broods and boils in loneliness,
For it remembers him.

Circle Of Stones

There is a place in High Park
Half hidden amongst the trees,
Where branches interlock
With bushes, shrubs, and weeds
Concealing narrow pathways
Leading to secluded places.
Follow the curving footpaths,
Try to remember them well,
Or probably you'll never be able
To find your way again.

It is a strangely quiet place
Perhaps it's hallowed ground
Mind not to break the spell,
Tread carefully, if you should wander near.
Though wild animals will peer round
From behind trees,
None will ever dare
Disturb the solitude

In the circle are slabs of stone,
Carved heads, with serene faces
Reminiscent of ancient people
Approach them with reverence
If you will,
For this is the park's sacred altar,
A secret Faire Ring.

The Beloved

I have distanced myself from those
I love most
My heart bleeds in an icy foreign land,
I flail against the stares of strangers,
Stares that inadvertently serve to conjure memories
That lie below a surface of unshed tears,
I cannot forget her
Jamaica, the land that shaped me, is my beloved,
She walks in balmy breezes,
Speaking tenderly in the hiss of her waterfalls,
She smolders in rippled fields of sugarcane,
Pungent mango groves, and in the hardy coconut palms
That bend like swans, where she juts out into the sea,
And that is where you ever will find me
Beneath the protective sky,
Heart joyfully reeling with sea birds
That squawk and twitter on the hot breeze,
Breezes that tempered me in its hands
Even as I and family clung together
Like slats of granite inseparable, or so we thought ...
Now distanced, I cannot forget the splendour
Shared momentarily
Like a tiny spark of flint against a flame,
For this is how it was.

Dying In Peru

Seven young men
Have died in Peru
Were you there that night in Lima
When the dancing started
And street lamps burned low
And the hand clapping escalated
In fiesta delight?
Were you part of the ecstasy
That tormented, terrified, and thrilled
In the nightclub room
Where those seven sons of Lima, with brave Inca faces
Faced the pallor of death,
To find their names carved
On the dark dance floor?
Did you see Juan, Pablo, Rico, Benito, Carlos, and Pedro
    fall?
Did they rip air from your breast,
And caused tears to cascade your warm cheeks,
And did you for one brief moment think of me
Millions of miles from the Andes
Giving thanks for your safety,
And shivering

Beckideed

Father, none of us
Can forget Beckideed,
The place you named
In our honour,
Using the first letters of all our names
As your marker,
And where, with your accountant's hands
You misguided, calculated the cooperation
Of soil, rocks, and weather
Hoping to rejoice in successful cultivation
Of coconut, banana, and sugarcane
On that dry barren land
That betrayed you, by resisting your additions and sub-
    tractions
Wanting more than you could afford to give,
Managing to entice you
With her show of wildness
That raged in the veins of her rivers and streams,
So wanton that it crushed your heart,
The boulder of all our fragile dreams,
And father, through the years
She haunts us all still,
Insinuating herself
With soft velvet whispers,
That like butterflies
On hibiscus flowers
linger.

Star Boys In J.A.

The evening, thick with crickets.
Frogs and mosquitoes give rise to ragged newspaper boys
Who shout "Star!" into the humid Kingston air.
They lean in at car windows,
Blue-black veins pumped up
From wanting the unattainable,
And their cheeks rounded
With lush Bombay and St. Julian seeds
That cannot disguise their melancholy eyes
Stained with dried blood tears
Of shame and regrets
Which seem to salivate even from the rusty zinc shacks
That totter on the verge of collapse at road's edge,
And the hissing sounds made in the Star boys' husky
    throats
Echo disconsolately, electrifying our attention,
And obliterate ragged sleeves,
Exposed knees, and inconsolable hopelessness.

Mermaid

Joseph, don't wake the dogs,
Don't send them scampering
Across this parched hot land,
For it is dangerous and dips into steep ravines
Where winds whistle incessantly
In banyan groves
And cry at the shoulders
Of mango and tamarind trees.
You must have heard the whispering.
The uproar, the clatter
Of the capricious quarrelling winds
That roam and weep
Under the starless sky
Where the moon walks in loneliness.
How I shiver, Joseph, my voice trembles
For well I know, I should not be here
Upon the terrible land,
For the night is full of threatening boulders
And ragged stones
Declaring danger at hand
For even in daylight hours
It supports the wandering
Of the sharp-horned, rib-exposed cattle
You love so well.

Slumber deep
While I outside your window
A vigil keep
Singing night's dark lullaby

To herald fireflies to light your way
With the coming of a Jamaican dawning,
When dirt tracks now concealed
Will be revealed
And hand holds can prevent
Dangerous slips, terrifying slides
Against the bramble, the wicked thorns
Where your bare feet kiss against loose soil.

Now, whistle up the dogs, Joseph
Your faithful companions strain to be leader and last
Of your mongrel pack.
The scent is on the wind,
Pointed ears thrust back,

Alive with barking and baying
In moonlight remembering.
Descend to the silver river bank
Of broad-leafed jungle splendour
Where float lily pads that glide
Like oil drops all a-shimmer.

Do not dally, Joseph,
Entice your companions on
To the lush vine-infested trees
The devilish overhangs
For in the perfection underneath,
We play hide and seek
In the still dark pools
And rushing water,
Nymph and fish in congregation
Clothed in water's silent rings
And in foam and in spray.

Joyous in moonlight's passing
Be not afraid, Joseph,
Draw near,
For I am here.

Jennifer's Room

Would that I had never
Crossed
The thresholds of her room,
Then I'd be reprieved
From haunting memories
Which play eternal inside my mind.
Shimmering they creep behind closed eyes
To fan the flames
That crackle and splutter
From their cave of logs,
Reflecting light off hard stones
Lining her rustic fireplace,
While casting shadows
Across the faerie ceiling.
Bold leaping tongues of light
Mesmerize in frenzied flutter,
Baiting her soft white quilts
To dance.
Would that I had never seen that room
With large low windows and views
That are no match
For interior hypnotic atmospheres
Where comfortable cushions
Strewn about
Invite attendance
At a throne.
And through the curtained glow,
Seek to conjure up places
Long explored, and
Making light of Arabian Nights,
While Jennifer lies dark-skinned

Against soft sheets
Being careful not to expose
Curves hidden in the
Folds of her bed clothes.
The low divan beside her bed
In its flamboyance
Teases the walls to race
And touch the ceiling.
There is a softness in
Her diamond eye

Which contests dreams, including
Mine,
Daring me, as it were
To usurp with one word,
The wonder
Reflected
In her room.

Edmund – My Father

As a child
You looked into the face of the sea
Where waves coiled, twisted, and lashed
Against the eye of the salty north coast wind,
And Edmund, what did you see?
How far did your thoughts fly?
We wonder,
Did you ever think of me?
Your future children
Left lonely and wandering

Were we first molded in sand and sweat,
With the scent of the sea,
And with hair that duplicated the flow
The sway, the rhythm of the dancing waves
Awash with weeds that flaunted
Upon the face of that sea?
And were our eyes ever as green as yours,
Or as pale as the distant horizon
That stretched silently
Into your far tomorrows
Beside the beach where you were born in Montego Bay?

And if I were to frequent that haunt
That exact location, the very indentation
Where you sat beneath racing clouds
Your thoughts taking ro ot like trees
In the hot white sand that blows a storm of memories yet
    to be,
I could be there precisely

Where broken boats are strewn
In the blazing sun to become
Wondrous wreckages, as white as bones,
While you gaze and dreamed,
Where something male in the cheek of the beach
The cut of its jaw, where it touches the reef
Now reminds me of you,
And where its fingers touch the shore,
Is that where you will be?

The Wind Will Not Walk Among Men Who Stand Still

If the howling wind comes calling,
Don't let him in,
Sorcery lives in him.
I've seen it in his eyes
Slanted like serpents in ecstasy,
I saw his lips pulled back
upon themselves with indulgent smiles.
He walks in my dreams,
My ignorant appreciative eyes
Measured his brawny thighs
And the long winding pillars and halls
Of his temples.
The wind will not drink of my blood red wine,
Though I bury ashes, eggshells and bones
To capture him.
He beats down my door
To break my heart with remembering,
The wind will not walk among men who stand still,
He will come with a roar and a riot.
Enchantment lives in the song he sings
As he weaves cloaks by moonlight,
And carves his name on window panes
Where men wait for miracles inside.
He is a gypsy howling wind,
His long black hair trails after him,
He speaks the language of the Tarot,
Scenting the air with fragrant wafts
Of rose and lavender.
The wind, the beguiling wanderer

Deludes all our senses
And in his practice,
Offers an enticing drink
Of his thick clotting honey
Of desire

I Am That Tree

I am that tree,
That grew outside your window,
Where my branches and leaves
Scrambled and scraped against
The smooth windowpanes
And rose and fell in gentle breezes,
And winds that wailed in fury,
To warn man, and beast, and birds,
Of dangers, and of hope in the coming
Wonder of the day ahead.

I am that tree that grew from a wild seed,
To become a sapling gold,
That shot towards the sky,
In two long summers
And though trimmed and cut many times,
I once again grew wild, as though resistant
To scissors and clippers,
As I rose again with pride,
Branches spread with leaves in clusters,
Trunk, crusty, broad, and beautiful,
As I shivered, unable to be still
Even for the nesting robin.

I am that tree,
That listened in,
To your telephone conversation,
About pesky critters
Raccoons, squirrels, and even wild birds
That used me as a stepping stone,
Or a ladder to the roof above your room,

Where the shingles were broken and destroyed.
And blamed on my proximity.

I am the tree that grew old,
And lost my majesty,
Even as I heard you speak so softly, almost tenderly,
To the man who could butcher me,
And strip me of my branches, my dried leaves my rotting
    trunk,
And you did not notice my shaking, my signalling,
For you never looked at me,
Though my leaves kissed each window pane,
And sighed in sad defeat.

I am that tree that could not hide,
When the blue truck came,
Moving slowly along the street,
As I heard the sound of nature's last song,
A sparrow's last call, as I mourned for myself

I am the tree
That was dismembered and sliced
Shoved into machinery that reduced me to sawdust parti-
    cles
That danced in the sunlit morn, when
The treeman made waste of me.

Dancing In The Sand

Don't write,
It clutters the brain,
Don't breathe, unless your pen
Allows it,
And if you move, move slowly.
Speak from the point of view
Of obscurity
And from that darkness,
Bring light.
Hold sounds in your hands,
Drip deep crescendos gently, one by one
From the tip of your pen,
Marvel at the crystal
That frees the wind from captivity,
And allows dancing in the sand.

We Children Grown

Now we are bent
 Like flowers in the wind,
Bent towards the graves
Where we will find rest
At the sides of the hills,
Those selfsame hills from
Our childhood days
Where we played,
Abandoning chores and the call
Of the ones who had needed us
To pause,
Even as we came trooping home
With voices high, splintering
The very sky,
Feeling triumphant with our every step,
Though now we are bent.

The Old Cane Chair

On the second floor
Of an abandoned house
Where bricks are gray and crumbling,
Sits an old cane chair.
Left there
Not far from a picture window
That forever looks out
From dust covered loneliness
To a garden below, bathed in light
Where foliage struggle for survival,
And the chair's plush cushions now gone flat
Are clothed with cobweb coverings
That sparkle in the intruding brilliance
Rendering designs of silken diamonds.
Reflected on broken window panes,
And the ragged curtain that once guarded,
No longer obscures the view below,
Where germination defies Fall's reckoning,
As Black-eyed Susans, bold and yellow sway
Alongside pale daisies and bright Primroses
That bow proudly in the Northern breeze,
Pretending to be unaware
Of the browning already started
On the surrounding leaves,
Though knowing they too will not last
Neither will the ferns,
The dancing Hollyhocks multihued, or the violets
Long past blossoming,
While the chair, as though attentive
In the quiet of that room's hush, observes

Grasses, shrubs and roses that forgot to bloom,
Cry out for attention
As the wind blows cold,
The air is chilled,
And the steadfast chair
Soon will lean,
Into the changing weather.

Effie

When Effie is alone
She hides behind
Lint, reels of thread, scattered bobbins
And sewing needles
That inhabit her existence.
She crouches over an ancient
Singer Sewing Machine,
Her bare feet firmly planted
On its pedal,
As with eyes closed,
And fingers trembling,
She knows she cannot afford
To service this once faithful, now aging
Tool.
She swallows brine against unfounded hope
In providence, and consumes the content
Of potent hundred proof mickies of rum,
That sting and burns her pallet,
And swiftly destroys her dreams
As her once attractive face, gives in
To the constant punishing.
Tears bleed down her crimson cheeks,
To water her scaly lips, her shoulders,
And at last the very hem of her frock
That she uses for drying and comforting,
Though it exposes her knobby knees,
That now alarms her,
For now, they are a testament,
To all that she has failed at,
  Conjuring remembrances,

Of the fashionable clothes,
She used to create for others
In this selfsame room,
Where she now fights for relevance

Previously Published

Kitchen Solitaire, Bite to Eat Place poetry Anthology Redwood Coast Press 1995. **Dying In Peru,** On line magazine, Jamaica No Problem (Chris Aguilar). **Mermaid,** Paperplates Magazine (Bernard Kelly) 1998. **Old Woman Things,** Revue Noire African Canada 1997. **Stone Woman,** Strong Winds Anthology 1997. **For Gwendolyn MacEwan,** Mentor's Canon Anthology 2001. **Dancing in the sand,** Set to music by Composer David Jaeger. **Edmund Our Father,** Heartbeat Anthology 2021. **The Face on Mars,** Polar Borealis Press online magazine 2021. **The Tenant Below,** Zygote magazine 1997. **Star Boys in J.A.,** An Invisible Accordion 1995. **In the Aftermath,** Tamaracks Canadian Poetry for the 21ᵗ Century 2018. **Where Sunlight Dare Not Follow,** Tamaracks 2018. **The Domino Players,** Mangrove Magazine, University of Miami 2004. **Night Journey,** Mangrove Magazine, University of Miami 2004. **The colours of my Adopted Country,** Mangrove Magazine, University of Miami 2004.

Some Selected Readings

2000, **Villa Fair**, at book sores in Vancouver, Kingston, Ottawa, and Montreal; 2004, **Waltzes I have not forgotten** at York University Hakka Chinese Conference; 2017-2018, Poetry at Open Mic Nights at Parliament Street Library; 2019, **Chasing the Banyan Wind**, at the Jamaican Consulate in Toronto; 2019, **Chasing the Banyan Wind** at the North York Centre; 2019, **Santiago's Purple Skies** at The Supermarket in Kensington Market; 2019, Nora Gold's Wonderful Women Writer's series; 2020, **Santiago's Purple Skies** at A Different Book List Book Store ;2021, **Lord of The Deep** on Zoom for the Cross Canada Storytellers Program.